Eco-tracking

Barbara Guth Worlds of Wonder

Science Series for Young Readers

Advisory Editors: David Holtby and Karen Taschek
Please see page 80 for more information about the series.

Eco-tracking

On the Trail of Habitat Change

DANIEL SHAW

WITH PHOTOGRAPHS BY MELANIE KEITHLEY,
JON LIVINGSTON MACLAKE,
AND THE AUTHOR

B O S Q U E S C H O O L

scholarship · community · integrity

University of New Mexico Press | Albuquerque

Printed in China by Four Colour Print Group

Production location: Guangdong, China | Date of Production 07/26/2010 | Cohort: Batch 1

15 14 13 12 11 10   1 2 3 4 5 6

Library of Congress Cataloging-in-Publication Data
Shaw, Daniel.
Eco-tracking : on the trail of habitat change / Daniel Shaw,
With photographs by Melanie Keithley, Jon Livingston MacLake, and the author.
p. cm. — (Worlds of wonder)
Includes index.
ISBN 978-0-8263-4531-8 (cloth : alk. paper)
1. Biotic communities—Juvenile literature.
2. Environmental awareness—Juvenile literature. I. Title.
QH541.14.S46 2010
577—dc22
2010010319

This book is dedicated to all young people who care for our planet and track environmental change, especially those in the Bosque Ecosystem Monitoring Program (BEMP), and of course my two favorite students of all time, Katie and Roland.

Contents

Acknowledgments

This book is the product of my time in the field with so many young friends and students. It is through our shared experiences of tracking environmental changes across our home landscape that I was able to write this book. I am particularly grateful to Albuquerque's Bosque School: its students, who trek into the woods with me through heat and snow; its board and administrators, who remain resolute that to fully develop, children need time in the out-of-doors; and my fellow teachers, who challenge our students and lead by example.

I am indebted to fellow teachers and environmental educators Cathy Bailey and Carolyn Espe for reviewing the manuscript so carefully and having taught me through the years how to be a better teacher, and to Colleen Seager for her production help and constant good cheer. My seventh-grade Bosque School students also reviewed the text and critiqued it with such great consideration and attention to detail that their English teacher, Ms. Hannaford, has earned my eternal respect for her excellence in teaching. Thanks, then, to my seventh-grade students Antonia, Dakota, Emily, Francesca, Jacob, Jared, Kiyomi, Lauren, Margaux, Quentin, Reilly, Sarintha, Sophie, Stuart, Tyler, and Will.

Finally, thanks to Clark Whitehorn and University of New Mexico Press as well as David Holtby and Karen Taschek, co-advisory editors of the Worlds of Wonder science series for young readers, for committing so firmly to expanded opportunities for young people to learn about and, more importantly, to engage with science.

Carefully observing even a common plant or animal provides a citizen scientist with useful information.

CHAPTER 1

Becoming a Citizen Scientist and Eco-tracker

Yesterday Katie looked right out her bedroom window and saw movement in the tree. There was a burst of gray fur. Then another. The first blur of fur chased the second from branch to branch, down to the ground, and then back into the tree. Movement stopped. Katie saw clearly that they were squirrels. And then, a moment later, the squirrels were wrestling on a tree branch without falling off. Katie reached for a beat-up old notebook. Last year she used it for math class. It still had blank pages in it when the year was done; this year, it holds all sorts of information about squirrels and rain and the wild world that blends into the city outside Katie's bedroom window. She wrote down the date, a comment about the weather, and a two-sentence description of what she observed. Today while sitting in the shade of the tree, Katie saw a hawk but no squirrels. Again she pulled out the old notebook and wrote what she saw and what she did not. Katie is a citizen scientist, an eco-tracker, and she is on the trail of changing habitat.

The **environment** is where you are. To be in **habitat** does not require a trip to Africa, a rain forest, or a national park. To discover the environment only requires that you pay attention to the world around you. It doesn't matter if you live in the busiest city in your state or if you are 50 miles from the nearest traffic light. You are surrounded by habitat, and it is constantly changing. To become an **eco-tracker** yourself, all you need to do is observe and record what you see today, what you see tomorrow, and what is different between those two points in time. Then you look for what caused that change. As an eco-tracker, you can work alone or with a few friends, a class, or thousands of people spread out across the country or even the world. You can keep the information yourself or you can share it with scientists who use what you see to better understand things like **global climate change** or how hawks **migrate**. When you share your findings with scientists, you become a **citizen scientist**. This book shows you how you can, as an eco-tracker and citizen scientist, learn about and care for a changing planet.

Habitat is everywhere, including faraway places like National Parks and National Forests.

First off, where do you live? What is your habitat? And how are you connected to the environment? Habitat is food, shelter, water, and space and how it is all arranged so that a creature can survive. The environment is everything in a place, including the weather, the land, the water, the chemicals in the air, and the germs in your breath. Each of us lives in the environment, and habitat surrounds us. To start off as an eco-tracker, it helps to know your own habitat and how you connect to the environment.

Habitat is also found right at home, like along a sidewalk or city street. Habitat is everywhere.

As living creatures, all people have habitat needs. To survive, both Katie and the squirrels she watched need food, water, shelter, and space. The trees outside her window met many of the squirrels' habitat needs. As people, Katie and you need more than just a few trees for habitat. How are your needs met? How big is your habitat? At first, it might seem small. Your bed, your kitchen, and your sink exist in the place of where you find most of your habitat needs. But is it really that small an area? How did the water get into your sink? Look under the sink. There are pipes. Those pipes connect to a water supply. Maybe you have a well right next to your house that pumps the water out of the ground for your family to use. Maybe you get your water from a stream or river that fills a 100,000-gallon (379,000-liter) neighborhood tank that then flows through the pipes to your house. In any case, the water comes from farther away than your sink, and your habitat area just expanded.

Katie's habitat stretches across the world. As the squirrels darted around the trees, Katie chomped on an apple. When she rinsed it off before she ate it, she had to peel off a tiny sticker. That little bit of paper and glue told her that the apple had come from New Zealand. A squirrel might go down the block to find food. Katie's apple traveled 8,700 miles (14,000 kilometers). People in the United States frequently eat food from all over the world. Especially in winter, food eaten in the United States often comes from South America or other distant places.

The food that is part of your habitat probably traveled great distances to reach you. Look on cereal boxes, cans of soup, and other food containers. Often you can find information about where the food came from. Those boxes and cans might also have a toll-free information telephone number. You can call the company up and ask someone where the company grows the food that it packages and sells. Again, what you think of as your habitat area is probably expanding far beyond just your kitchen or your local grocery store.

Well, at least the shelter of your bed doesn't stretch your habitat across the country or around the world. Or does it? How is that area kept warm in the winter and cool in the summer? Does your family have heating and air conditioning? If so, where does the energy come from for that temperature control? Is it from electricity created by burning coal? Is it from gas burning in a furnace? If so, the warm shelter of your habitat might stretch all the way across an ocean and into the oil fields of a faraway country.

Your habitat may stretch across the whole planet. The squirrels Katie watched out her bedroom window may have a habitat that is no bigger than a soccer field. The hawk that landed in the same tree in which the squirrels were wrestling may have spent the previous month 3,100 miles (5,000 kilometers) away in Mexico. Yet Katie, the squirrels, and the hawk all share habitat. Each day the habitat and environment outside Katie's window is different. Sometimes it's wildly different. As an eco-tracker, Katie carefully observed these changes. She recorded how in one night an ice storm damaged the tree. It caused huge, jagged branches to fall to the ground. Even on days when the tree seems the same, Katie makes careful observations. She takes time to notice one new twig on the ground let loose from the squirrel's nest overhead or a few leaves chewed by caterpillars. To be an eco-tracker, one looks for what stays the same and for what changes.

The ability to make connections between things that at first seem separate is at the heart of eco-tracking. Nothing stands alone. How does a button become part of a coat? How does a sparrow become part of your life? What is the thread that holds the button to the fabric? What is the connection that links a little bird to your world?

Habitat can be one twig when cottonwood beetle larvae use it to survive.

This is how an eco-tracker thinks. First you see something. Then you ask, "Why is it here and not there? What is different between this place and that? If I wait and watch, will it move into that place too? Why or why not? What is it about this place that makes some living thing able to survive here? What interacts with it? What will it look like later when summer's heat takes over this place? What else will change because this changes?"

Say you are playing soccer. You stop for a moment to have a snack. Some crumbs fall to the ground. You go back to your game. A small brown sparrow flies down and starts eating the crumbs of your snack. Ants haul off the crumbs not claimed by the sparrow. As the ants harvest crumbs, a lizard comes along and laps up some of the ants. You have just connected the meal of your habitat with that of three other **species**, or particular type of plant or animal. As you walk home from your soccer game, you cut across a vacant field. Grasshoppers stir and jump as you pass. An American kestrel, a small falcon, swoops down and kills and eats a grasshopper startled by your movement. Your movement causes the death of one animal and the survival of another.

There are all sorts of connections within the environment. For example, nitrogen is a natural chemical in animal waste. The waste falls to the ground, say, as a deer's urine and it becomes part of the mineral soil. Minerals in the soil enrich a plant and permit it to grow. The deer then feeds on the nourished plant, and the connections circle. But what happens to the plant when there is no deer? Sure, it's not being eaten by the deer, but is the plant healthy without the rich mineral soil? It doesn't have to deal with deer feeding on it, but is it still healthy enough to fight off disease or insects?

So if one patch of soil, a plant, and a deer are all linked, what else is connected? You can look at any small patch of earth as an

ecosystem and then start expanding your view from there. A fallen log, the damp soil under a rock, one tree with a bird's nest, or your own backyard can be the start of your ecosystem exploration. From there you build out. A flowerpot on your front porch is an ecosystem. This flowerpot no bigger than a basketball connects with the world. When a bee carries pollen from the flower in that pot back to its hive, the ecosystem you are looking at can stretch out over two miles (three kilometers) from your front porch. Small habitats link and become communities, communities merge and become whole **bioregions**, and bioregions link and become the earth.

What happens in your own neighborhood is linked with the whole world. Sometimes what links people around the world is easy to understand. For example, each summer the Swainson's hawk can be found eating mosquitoes and other insects in many areas of the United States. When winter comes, these birds fly to Argentina and other areas in South America where it's warm during that time of the year and insects are abundant. However, it's more difficult to understand how our use of cars to travel to the mall can change how hard or how easy it is for a polar bear to hunt a seal. Exhaust from many cars zipping to the mall and elsewhere can affect the weather and climate in the Arctic. This exhaust can add to changes causing arctic ice to melt. Polar bears use the ice as their hunting habitat. The melting ice reduces a polar bear's hunting habitat and success and threatens its survival.

Car exhaust is just one part of our waste stream. Each living thing on this planet alters its environment as it survives. An elk chewing off clumps of grass, a cactus drawing water up through its roots, and a turtle digging into the mud at the bottom of a pond are changing the environment around them. How much of an impact a living thing has on the environment can be thought of as a footprint. If you walk

Map Your Habitat

Supplies needed: Paper and pencil, map of the world, phone book, telephone, or computer with Internet service

How big is your habitat? First make a list of the following parts making up habitat: food, water, shelter, space, and energy. Trace several things that make up that habitat backward from your house to their source in the earth. For example, if you write under the *food* part *chocolate-coated, honey-dipped, sugar wheat flakes breakfast cereal*, you need to find out where the cereal manufacturer gets its ingredients. You are finding out where that food is from because it may be a combination of ingredients from different places. To find this information, look on the package for a description of where the food is grown or raised. If it isn't there, look for a toll-free consumer information phone number or website on the package. You can either call the phone number or contact the company through their website and ask where the ingredients are grown or raised. Do this for several types of your food.

Then do the same thing for your energy and water needs. Your local water and energy utilities probably send monthly bills to your family. The bills have phone numbers. Call those numbers and ask to speak to someone in the utilities' public relations or education department. These people can help explain where the utilities get the water or energy they send to you and your family. Tracking down the source of your shelter will probably be harder. Find out from a local building supply store where the store gets the wood and other supplies it sells to people who construct homes.

along a sandy beach, you leave a track in the soft sand. Our **environmental footprint** is a description of the changes we leave on the land, water, and air as we live on this planet.

There is tremendous concern around the world about how much of a collective environmental footprint all of the people on this planet have on the earth. This planet is now home to over 6 billion people. Each of us draws water to use and consumes food and energy. How we do that and what our waste stream looks like defines our environmental footprint. There are things we do that reduce our environmental footprint. We can recycle instead of throwing recyclable items into the trash. For short trips, we can walk instead of riding in a car. When possible, we can eat food from local farms. We can enhance the habitat around us by helping to clean up a local stream on National River Cleanup Week or just by planting flowers to create butterfly habitat. These decisions in our everyday lives make a difference in the world around us.

As you begin to understand your habitat and environmental changes,

Each of us has an environmental footprint based on the energy, food, and other resources we use.

Map Your Neighborhood's Wild Habitat

Supplies needed: Paper and pencil

You can draw a neighborhood habitat map. If a bird flew over your house, what would it see? Put your house in the center of the map. Where are the nearest trees, grassy areas, flowers, and bushes? Put those on your map. You don't need a forest to find habitat. One tree or one bush becomes home to many small animals. Where does water flow from your house when it rains? Draw the water's path, even if it only flows there sometimes. Are there any streams, puddles, or other watery areas nearby? Put those on your map. Where there's water, there's life. If you have green places like parks, wooded areas, or fields, does anything link them? Even a dirt path with some weeds along it can link two habitat areas. Are there big barriers, like roads, fences, and concrete walls between small habitat areas? If so, put those on your map too.

you will begin to see links. You will see how the water you drink and use at your home connects you with the fish in a nearby stream. As your view stretches out, you will see how a tree blocking the wind on the north side of your school not only cuts down on your school's energy use, but also creates habitat for a family of robins and provides some cool summer shade for you to hang out and visit with friends.

As you become more of an eco-tracker, you will build a spiderweb of understanding. You will discover what keeps an environment healthy over time and what harms it. As an eco-tracker, you will see connections

To draw a map of your local area's habitat, include where animals can find food, shelter, and water.

Sustainable Living

The ability to live in one place over time is called *sustainable living*. It means your energy, food, and water supplies are used only in a way that allows them to be recharged and to be available for hundreds of years or longer. Another important part of sustainable living has to do with your waste stream. After your needs are met, the waste you generate as trash, dirty water, and exhaust is able to be recycled in your home area in a healthy way. It doesn't poison your water or air supply or otherwise harm your environment. If your living practices are sustainable over time, you can describe your environmental footprint on the earth as being small and "green."

In New Mexico, there are Native American communities called Pueblos. Long before Columbus and other Europeans came to what is now the United States, Puebloan people lived in farming communities throughout New Mexico. Many of those Pueblos still thrive today in their exact same places. For example, in northern New Mexico people have lived on Taos Pueblo lands for over a thousand years. Their homes are considered to be the oldest continuously lived-in communities in the United States. To do that requires the ability to have a green environmental footprint and to live in a sustainable manner.

A few miles away from Taos Pueblo is another sustainable community. It is the Earthship Biotecture community, where people build and live in homes that are as sustainable as people can think to make them. The houses heat and cool themselves using solar energy and the earth itself. The water they use comes from rain and snowmelt. After being used in

and find changes. You will find out how you connect with and care for your local environment and the earth. Furthermore, you will discover how your local environment and earth connect with

and sustain you. As a citizen scientist, you will combine your work with that of others to help care for the shared habitat of all humans and other life on earth.

Young people can measure local environmental conditions and become citizen scientists by sharing their results.

the home, the water helps to grow much of the food the families eat.

As you explore how the people in your home, neighborhood, and community meet their habitat needs of food, water, shelter, and energy, think about and ask if those practices are sustainable. Will your community be able to meet its water and energy needs in 25 or 100 years in the same way it does now? If so, what are the sustainable practices allowing your community to meet those needs? If not, what will need to be done to help your community make a green and sustainable footprint? What can you do in your own home to keep your own environmental footprint green and small?

A raven is at adult size when it leaves the nest.

CHAPTER 2

Out Your Door and into the Environment

Diego wasn't doing much. He was just waiting for a ride. As he sat in front of his school, he saw a pair of big black birds. Their beaks were huge and thick. They sat side by side on top of two lampposts. One had its neck stretched out and was calling. The other said nothing. Diego didn't know what kind of birds they were or what name scientists would call them. At this point, he just knew they were black and big. The silent one flew down to the ground and started to eat something. The noisy one followed and got even noisier. Diego just sat still and watched. From his spot, he could see the noisy one open its red mouth. It spread out its wings a little and turned its head upward. To Diego, it seemed that the noisy one was trying to beg food from the quiet one. Wherever the silent one went to eat, the noisy one followed and begged. Diego wondered if the noisy one was hurt. He watched carefully. It didn't seem to be hurt. It moved exactly like

the quiet one except it begged instead of picking up food. He wondered if it was a baby. He looked closely. It was the same size as the quiet one. If it was a baby, it was a big baby. At that point, a car drove along and the birds flew off. Diego pulled out a notebook. He wrote down the date, time, location, and what he saw. He drew a little sketch of the birds and how the two stood in relation to each other while one begged and the other fed. The art wasn't fancy. In a moment, Diego's ride showed up and he, like the big black birds, left.

A **naturalist** is someone who studies nature. Since the environment is everywhere, there is always nature to see. Of course, a pond at a nature center or a mountain meadow in a national park might have loads of wild things to see, but so does a city street or a schoolyard. It's just a matter of looking. It doesn't matter where you look; it just matters that you look. When Diego watched the two birds along a city street, he was a naturalist. When he wrote down what he saw, he became a scientist. If he goes back to that place and watches for those birds and records how the situation there has changed, he becomes an eco-tracker. To become a citizen scientist, Diego needs to share his findings with other researchers.

Science isn't science until it's recorded. Seeing something in nature may be interesting or even exciting, but for you to be part of a scientific investigation, you must carefully record what you observe. Good science requires that you only record the facts. For example, Diego could write in his **field notes**, *Loud bird did not seem to be hurt*. He didn't do a full medical exam of the bird so he couldn't write, *Loud bird was not hurt*. The more detail you add to your observations, the better. It's always hard to say what recorded information will become the most helpful in answering a question. Always add as much detail to your field notes as possible.

A core and essential part of science is to objectively record what you observe and discover.

There are many ways of recording information. Diego did the simplest: he wrote something down. But he could have also used a camera, a computer data logger, or a digital sound recorder. All of these are tools used by scientists to record what they detect and observe. Using sketches to show how one thing relates to another is helpful. Diego drew a sketch in his field notes to show the relationship between the two birds he saw.

Simple drawings can be done quickly and record important information. Diego can show where a bird's nest is in a tree by doing something as simple as drawing an X on what looks like a lollipop. The lollipop is the tree and the X is the nest. To make it a helpful scientific drawing, all Diego's drawing needs is a key. A key shows what each symbol represents. It helps someone else look at a picture and understand what it means. In Diego's case, the key will help him remember, over time, what his drawing shows.

Maintaining a Field Journal

The difference between an eco-tracker and someone carefully looking at the environment is that an eco-tracker records what is seen. A simple and inexpensive way to record observations is with a field journal. A field journal can be a notebook or a blank diary book. It can be as big as a sketch pad or as small as a wallet. Each field journal is unique, but the scientific guidelines for creating them remain the same. Each time you write in a field journal, it's called making an entry. Each entry should start with the date, time of day, location, and summary about the weather. What makes up the rest of the entry depends on what is being examined.

The more detail you add to your notes, the better. However, what you put in your journal should be true and free of prejudice. Or, as scientists say, it should be *accurate* and as bias free as possible. Be *precise*. If you see a flock of geese, try and count them to record, *12 geese*; if you only have a chance to count 10 geese but you know there were more, write, *at least 10 geese*. The details, precision, and accuracy of your notes help you make scientific comparisons and observations through a strong field journal.

Words and numbers are just the start of a good field journal. Sketches and diagrams enhance your recorded information. It might be far easier and quicker to show the pattern on a turtle's shell with a sketch than to do it using only words. A science journal is not so much about the art as it is about the information. Some of the most artistic expressions of nature are found in field journals. Details in

A date, the name of a species observed, and simple drawings may not seem like much at all. Yet sometimes such information becomes part of a much larger environmental understanding. This is exactly what happened when the field records from many observers showed that on average, tree swallows have been laying their eggs earlier each year. Similar work by many naturalists show that the Edith's checkerspot butterfly is moving farther north and to taller mountains to find cooler conditions. Both the tree swallow and Edith's checkerspot butterfly are examples of how citizens can gather information to help track changes in global climate conditions. Citizen science does not need to be fancy; it just needs to be trustworthy.

In science, you can't change the results or alter a situation just to meet your wish. For example, if you were trying to see what kind of seeds ants are gathering on a certain day, you can't hide all of the blue seeds under a rock and when the ants take the red seeds say they like red seeds better than blue. When you decide what your answer will be before you see the facts, you're being prejudiced. In science, a prejudice is called a **bias**. Scientists try very hard to avoid letting biases into their studies. By sitting still while watching the birds, Diego tried not to cause the birds to act differently than they otherwise would if he hadn't been there. To keep his notes bias free, he recorded only what really happened.

Sometimes our actions do cause results to change. For example, you could stand up and startle a rabbit you're watching. Sometimes you might not be sure if you did something to alter the results. This could be the case if you were watching the rabbit and it ran off just as you stood up and a dog went past. Maybe the rabbit moved because of you, the dog, or both you and the dog. It would be hard to say exactly what caused the rabbit to move. In your notes, you write how you, the dog, or maybe both of you together might have changed the results. Of course, something else like hunger or thirst could have caused the rabbit to move. It's important that you record what happened and anything that could have altered what took place.

Being an eco-tracker only starts with field observations. There is always plenty to explore inside as well as out. Once Diego got to a computer or a library, he could look for more information about

science enhance details in art. Journals can also be a great place to tape in a leaf or other piece of nature to help you explain or remember your nature observation.

Quality and important citizen science often involves only simple and inexpensive tools like rulers, notebooks, and a pen.

Identification books, like a field guide to birds, can be of great help to a citizen scientist.

what he saw. On a computer, he could use a search engine like Google and type in *bird identification*. He might go to a library and use a special book called a **field guide** for identifying animals, plants, and other things found in nature. In either case, his sketch and comments about the birds' size, color, and behavior will help him figure out that he was watching a pair of ravens.

If he looks up additional information about ravens and their behavior, Diego will find out that the red mouth means the noisy raven was not yet an adult. Diego could also find out that all songbirds, including ravens, are fully grown in size when they leave the nest. After thinking about both what he observed and what science has already recorded about ravens, Diego could figure out that probably he was watching a parent teaching a very young raven how to find its own food.

What Diego observed might not be new to science, but it was new to him. It may be new to science if he saw ravens in an area where no one else had ever seen them or it was the earliest date a young raven was ever seen out of a nest in that particular area. One baby bird of one species found hopping around outside a nest in early spring might not mean that much. But if many naturalists were noticing baby birds of many different species out and about earlier than ever, that might mean a great deal. It could be because of a changing global climate or some other large ecological change.

One person's observations can be important. The observations of many different people combined can be very important. Now, through the Internet, there are ways for ordinary people, no matter how young or old they are, to work with scientists and to study ecosystem changes. These programs range from watching for the first signs of spring to record-ing all the birds you can identify in your area at the end of December. These efforts are called **citizen science programs**. Anyone who is a careful observer can help out with these projects.

There are all sorts of citizen science programs, including many that examine common animals like pigeons.

Citizen science programs offer a great way to expand on or get started with eco-tracking. First of all, you can pick out a topic interesting to you and practical for your area. If you live along a busy city street in an apartment and like birds, you can participate in something like Pigeon Watch and work with scientists from Cornell University. If you're interested in global climate change, you can tie into a worldwide study conducted by students and other people of all ages researching weather and climate through the Global Learning

Keeping Species Lists

Many eco-trackers and naturalists like to keep **species lists**. A species list is the record of different types of species one observer sees. Along with the species name, the naturalist writes the location of the observation and date. These lists can cover different time periods. A **daily list** describes only those species seen in a day. A species list kept throughout a person's life is called a **life list**. One kept for a year is an **annual list**. One kept that just covers one particular place is called an **area list**. These lists can include different types of species or one category or class of species, like birds or trees.

Like in all science, it is important to record only what you know to be true in a species list. Just because you want to see 25 species of birds in one day, you can't call a flash of red in the trees an American robin if you aren't able to verify several characteristics specific to a robin. This might mean knowing the robin's song and hearing it, knowing its shape as well as its color, and learning its pattern of flight. Good field guides will help you learn how to do that. Other sources of information include rangers at local nature centers and parks and members of nature groups like the Audubon Society or a local native plant club.

An annual area list allows an eco-tracker to make comparisons between years. One comes to understand what is common and what is rare for a particular place. An annual list also allows someone to see how the environment is changing. The animals and plants found in one place can change over time as habitat and other conditions change.

and Observations to Benefit the Environment (GLOBE) program. These programs, and many others, are set up for you to record information in your neighborhood and send it to scientists who post your findings on the web.

In a citizen science program, your information becomes part of larger studies conducted by real scientists.

A citizen scientist looking at the micro-view can discover much by observing small details and looking closely at the environment at hand.

The information you collect is called **data**. Citizen science programs have **protocols**, or procedures, that tell you how to gather the data. By gathering the information in a certain way, people all over the world can compare what is taking place in their neighborhood with what is happening in your area. The protocols, necessary **data forms**, and directions for submitting your data are often found on easy-to-follow websites. Some programs are free, while others require membership and/or equipment costs. Citizen science programs like these can involve thousands of eco-trackers.

Eco-trackers can also work alone. They can set up their own study of an area or of any plants or animals within an area. Eco-trackers can create their own data collection protocols and forms. They can look at their own information to make their own reports. There is no one right way to be an eco-tracker. Countless paths into the environment are rich with adventure and opportunity.

Eco-trackers can look at something huge or small. They might look at a whole forest or just one tree or switch back and forth between the two. They can watch how one beetle moves through a field of grass or they can look at the whole field. When you look at something up close, it is called a **micro-view**. When you look at something from a distance, it's called a **macro-view**. Sometimes the micro-view explains the macro-view and sometimes it's the other way around. Each view tells you about the other.

When Diego was younger, as part of a citizen science program, he studied a forest that had burned. Remarkably, where he studied was just as interesting as what he studied. His project looked at how cottonwood trees survived after a forest fire. Fireworks had started the fire, and it burned through a city park and just a few yards (meters) from the city zoo and its polar bears. As Diego and his friends gathered data about their wild-forest study area, they could see polar bears looking down on them from the high spot of the bear enclosure. Diego and his friends looked up from their work and saw the bears and the whole area surrounding them.

On the micro-level, they saw how a tree that had survived the fire had many small insects, like aphids, feeding on its new leaves.

Reading the Land

Across the land, there are millions of clues. Clues build into stories. These stories hold the history of the land. There are people who can read the land and know what happened as easily as someone can read a newspaper to find out about yesterday's baseball game. Reading the land is a skill. As you practice this skill, you will get better and faster at figuring out what events took place on the land.

Wind and water are just two forces of nature. Both of them leave their mark on the environment. You can find their impacts on a whole forest or on just one tree. A tree might be taller than its neighbors because it's near a stream where its roots can get the water it needs to grow taller. The same tree might lean a bit to the north because most of the time winds push against it from the south.

In your own neighborhood, you can look for and find all sorts of environmental clues. Looking for clues can lead you down a trail. You can find where a deer bit off a branch and then walked across deep mud and left tracks. You can see how the mud exists in a place where a stream used to run higher and how the extra water pushed down and flattened some plants. Each observation links to another. Your discovery of clues will help you read the land as easily as you read this sentence.

As Diego looked up and around, he saw other burned trees with heavy infestations of aphids. A short distance away, he saw that the unburned trees didn't have the insects. Diego's macro-view showed him the contrast of burned and unburned trees as related to aphids. This information became part of his citizen science field notes.

Diego saw the difference, but he didn't know what caused the burned trees to be fed on by insects and the unburned ones to be left alone. It takes a careful eco-tracker not to jump to conclusions and bias his or her answer. That is why eco-trackers record what is there, not what they expect to be there. In this case, Diego had to do some more investigation. Through reading, he learned that aphids are found on both healthy and unhealthy trees. However, he also learned that these tiny insects, with their straw-like mouths, could swarm and suck nutrients from a stressed tree. Diego realized that even though the trees had survived the fire, they were damaged and vulnerable to insects and other threats like disease.

Diego carefully looked at tiny details on individual leaves. He also looked at the whole forest. It meant shifting back and forth between the macro- and micro-views.

A burned forest offers tremendous opportunity to see change. The ground around a freshly burned tree is often black. If the fire was very recent, life is sometimes hard to find. Several months after a fire, green plants often come up through the blackened ground. Over time, the ground's black color changes. In time, the only black remaining exists on tree trunks and large chunks of wood that once burned. For Diego, he was recording the story of how a fire changed a forest.

To be a careful observer, you must look at both the object you are studying and its surrounding environment. After you see the conditions in one little area, lift your eyes and look. Does the pattern in one area repeat itself across a larger area? If it repeats, does it look exactly the same or slightly different? If it's unique, what patterns surround that unique area and how are the adjacent areas different?

Recording information after a fire or other change to an area can provide scientists with important information.

Discovering patterns is a big part of discovering nature. Are certain types or species of trees only growing along riverbanks? You can also use your other senses to discover patterns. Can you hear certain bird noises only when a dog, coyote, fox, or other predator is nearby? Do honeybees visit only strong-smelling flowers? To be a successful eco-tracker scientist, you must search out connections between different parts of the ecosystem. That searching can take place without traveling very far at all.

One can discover all sorts of information about the earth in a very small area. In your neighborhood, a short walk around the block can reveal where small sparrows fly for shelter, where water collects after a rainstorm, and if openings to anthills are more likely to face south and toward the sun or north and away from the sun. Do remember, the difference between just taking a walk and being a scientist is making sure observations are carefully recorded.

To move from being a scientific naturalist to an eco-tracker, one must watch one part of the environment over time. You can study just one animal or a whole forest or field. The important thing is to see how it stays the same and how it changes. Eco-trackers can observe one pigeon nest on a building's ledge. They can watch it over five to six weeks from the time the mother starts sitting on the eggs until the young fly away. There are different questions to ask and answers to learn through careful observations. How often are the young left alone? What happens in bad weather? Do the young change their behavior when cars and trucks go past? How many survive and how many die?

A nest full of pigeons might keep some eco-trackers busy for a month or so, but a field might keep them busy for years. A field, left alone, can easily turn into a forest. It might take many years to do so. Eco-trackers who study one place over the long term can chart out change and understand why it becomes one type of place and not another.

Eco-tracking and citizen science projects can take a week or a lifetime. Projects can take place in a city, along a riverbank, in a park or schoolyard, on a farm, or in a wilderness area. The study site can stretch out just an arm's length or across many states or countries. It can be the work of one person or many. Plants, birds, insects, the weather, or any other part or parts of the environment can be the study's focus. What matters most is that there is a careful, unbiased observer recording what is seen today and what is seen tomorrow.

Climate, a description of the weather over time, is a long-term and steady ecological driver.

CHAPTER 3
Ecological Drivers Change Habitat

To Roland, it seemed a bulldozer had made this mess in the middle of the night. Yesterday this had been a forest grove. He had walked right through it in just a few minutes. This morning there were a dozen twisted cottonwood stumps and fallen trees. To travel across this grove now required climbing and crawling and more time than he had to spare. There had been no bulldozer. No road led in or out of this part of the forest. Humans hadn't caused this. It was nature itself. It had been the wind. Yesterday afternoon wind came in from the west sounding like a freight train. The wind blew over 50 miles per hour (80 kilometers per hour). Branches fell down all over town, and several neighborhoods lost electrical power. Now this part of the forest didn't even look like the same place it was yesterday. Even with all the change, Roland still saw life. A dozen birds fed at the base of an uprooted tree. Although many cottonwoods were down, many still stood. This forest had changed, yet still it lived.

The wind wasn't the first big change to hit Roland's forest grove. Three years earlier, a forest fire had burned there. This area was next to Roland's school, and through the years, Roland saw life thriving there. In between the fire and windstorm, Roland had seen bald eagles and Cooper's hawks, coyotes and rabbits, new wild-flowers and shrubs, and giant old trees that somehow survived the fire. Nature is never dull. There are constant forces in motion; life responds. Fire, flood, and weather are all examples of **ecological drivers**. Ecological drivers are forces acting on the environment and causing change.

You can think of ecological drivers as drivers of different vehicle types on a city street. A trash truck comes along and scoops up waste. A bunch of semi-trucks hauling heavy loads of gravel crush down on the road. School buses pick up and drop off passengers. When a thousand people in a thousand cars head off to work at the same time, they can clog up a road. In the forest, a small fire can clean things up by burning accumulated sticks and branches on the forest floor. Strong winds wear down rocks through erosion and pick up and drop seeds, branches, and even trees. A flood can scoop up objects in one place, carry them a distance, and drop them off far away. Even a changing climate can cause changes by creating a carbon-rich atmosphere, where plants grow more quickly.

In each of these cases, the ecological driver pushes the ecosystem in one way or another and the land changes because of these forces. Sometimes one particular ecological driver is dominant. It has the greatest influence on a particular habitat for a long period of time. In this case, plants and animals living there **adapted** to surviving under conditions created by that ecological driver.

Roland was familiar with one of North America's most important ecological drivers: fire. Not only had he seen fire's impact along the river and near his school, he had also seen it in a mountain area not

Floods can cause erosion in short periods and reshape the land.

far from his home. In the mountains, fire had burned in a ponderosa pine forest.

When Roland first visited the mountain area after the fire, he saw many dead trees and a vast area of blackened ground. Over the next several years, he saw how the trees that survived grew taller and the blackened ground became covered in grasses and wildflowers. What he saw was normal. For thousands of years, every three to seven years, a light forest fire would burn through ponderosa forests. Twigs, pine needles, and other materials on the forest floor would burn. Some ponderosa pines died, but many survived. Although fire would kill some individual plants, the entire forest would be healthier. Surviving trees had better access to nutrients released into the soil by the fire. They had less chance of getting diseases since they weren't living in overly crowded conditions.

The ponderosa pine trees and the other plants and animals that survived in these locations became fire adapted. That is, as

top: A forest fire can rapidly kill most everything aboveground.

bottom: If a forest has evolved with fire, it can quickly spring back to life in a month or less after a fire moves through it.

populations of plants and animals, they survived and were healthy. Roland saw that process as he watched that area recover.

In recent times, the pattern of low-intensity and frequent fires has changed in many ponderosa pine forests. For most of the past 100 years, people kept many ponderosa pine forests from burning. This happened through human firefighting efforts and other changes. At one time, fires could quickly spread and burn lightly across grassy forest floors. Removal of grasses by overgrazing and drought makes it harder for light fires to happen. The buildup of many years of dead branches and trees leads to hot, intense fires that kill large sections of forest. It's natural for these forests to burn because one of their main ecological drivers is fire. If fire is removed for too long, other ecological drivers like disease and forest insect outbreaks occur. When there is a fire, it's huge, hotter, and more destructive than the light fires of before.

In Roland's riverside forest in Albuquerque, New Mexico, several different types of ecological drivers exist. Ten thousand years ago, a wall of glacial ice scoured the river valley where the Rio Grande now flows. The bare ground left by the glacier became the place where Roland's forest grew. As the cottonwood trees grew, they created the forest now known by its Spanish name, **bosque**. Each spring, as mountain snows melted, the river grew in size. For many years, so much snow melted, the river would spread over its banks and flood. When it flooded, it deposited rich river soil. Regular flooding allowed new cottonwood trees to sprout from sandy beaches. Forest debris, like leaves and logs, was either washed away or buried in river mud. For all of these years, flooding was the Rio Grande and its riverside forest's major ecological driver.

In the past 50 years, a new ecological driver has emerged in the bosque: fire. Long kept out of the area by moist soils and other impacts of flooding, fire has taken advantage of new conditions. In recent years, dams and levees built to reduce and control flooding have dried out soils and allowed for the buildup of dead plant material on the forest floor. Cottonwood tree seeds don't easily sprout and survive in non-flooded soil. They are out-competed by the **exotic**, fire-loving tamarisk and Russian olive trees. Fire is replacing flooding as the ecological driver and is transforming the river valley and Roland's bosque.

All ecosystems have multiple ecological drivers. **Climate**, the long-term weather conditions of a place, is always an ecological driver. Other drivers come into play depending on where an ecosystem is. In Roland's forest, the drivers are fire and flood. In Florida or Hawaii, drivers might include ocean storms like hurricanes and geological events like volcanic eruptions and tsunamis.

Having multiple ecological drivers in an ecosystem is like having more than one cook in the kitchen. The cooks all might be grabbing food from the same cabinets and refrigerator, but each of them takes the ingredients and acts on them in a different way. Some make delicate pastries and others hearty loaves of bread. The results vary depending on who is doing the cooking. Some items flourish, others rot, and some remain untouched in the cupboard. How an ecosystem looks depends on what is doing the ecological driving.

A large hailstorm can alter environments in a short time.

To understand an ecosystem, it is important to understand its ecological drivers. In many stable systems, the same ecological drivers can sculpt a particular ecosystem for tens of thousands of years or longer. Of course, things could change tomorrow. It's also important to remain open to the idea that the ecological drivers of today may not have been the ecological drivers of yesterday.

People often think only in the present. They see something and think, *That is how it is and how it was and how it will be.* Of course, they notice drastic change, like a tornado ripping up a patch of forest or down their main city street. An eco-tracker notices gradual changes, just like Roland noticed the recovery and regrowth of the mountain forest. Some changes take a long time and are hard to see, like when a meadow takes 30 years or more to become a forest. Even so, it's important that eco-trackers look at and record environmental changes. To be an eco-tracker, one must possess the ability to see a situation across time and to notice changes, even very small-step changes.

Change is a part of all life. It might be good. It might be bad. It might just be change. When you were born, you were small. Now you're larger. If you looked at a picture of yourself when you were born and one from today, you would easily see the change. If you

looked at a series of pictures of yourself from every day of your life from birth to today, the changes would appear more gradual.

Tracking down causes that lead to changes can be both easy and difficult. Seeing how a forest is changed by fire is easier than seeing how it is changed by global climate conditions. Ecological drivers are both local and global. There are things that happen right where you are that cause changes right there in that spot. You can easily see how a beaver building a dam blocks a stream and creates a mountain pond. It's more difficult to see how warm ocean temperatures in the South Pacific Ocean create winter snowstorms in the southwestern United States, eventually filling that beaver pond with water from melting snow. Both the beaver and warming ocean temperatures are ecological drivers in that mountain meadow.

If the soils around the beaver pond stay moist because of heavy snows, then a water-loving plant like a cattail has a better chance of surviving than a dry-soil plant like a cactus. Each plant or animal has an ideal range of conditions for survival. It might be able to live in an area outside of its best conditions, but it won't thrive. There are groups, or **communities**, of plants and

Infrared cameras can capture the nighttime work of how beaver transform habitats.

animals that thrive together. They are adapted and well suited to the primary ecological drivers of an area.

In your neighborhood, explore and look for signs of ecological drivers. Some will be obvious and others hidden from view. Some ecological drivers might be left over from long ago while others occurred last week. Start your exploration by looking at the soils and rocks and their arrangement. The earth's surface creates the first layer for whatever habitat in that area is possible. From rocks come soils; from soils come plants. Not all soils support all types of plants. Golden bladderpods thrive in soil rich in lime and sandstone made from corals, shellfish, and ocean sands from millions of years ago. But the still stranger-sounding Mogollon whitlowgrass grows quite well in scraps of soil between volcanic lava flows from just several hundred years ago.

The steady flow of water and wind can cause erosion by wearing away soil.

It's not just the earth's rocks and soils that determine what can live where. The shape of the land also permits or limits different habitat types. Tiny bits of rock, soil, and other sediments quickly wash down a steep cliff, but a flat valley below allows sediments to build up and enrich the land for vegetation to grow. The wearing away of rocks and other sediments by wind and water is known as **erosion**. Erosion can be a powerful ecological driver. Erosion creates a rich and fertile belt of land around where rivers flood. Look around your neighborhood for places where the earth's surface is being cut away by erosion. Also, look for places where sediments are being deposited and making life possible.

Of course, erosion has another side too. When erosion mixes with the ecological drivers of drought and human-caused changes like overgrazing, whole areas can be turned to desert. This process of **desertification** takes place across the world and converts areas the size of South Carolina into desert each year.

Drought, hurricanes, winds, temperature, and rain are all part of weather. To know your local habitat, you need to know the weather. Not just today, but across time. When you look at weather over time, you're studying the climate. In addition to soils, climate is a tremendous factor in what grows and survives in a specific area. It's important to keep track of weather information in your field journal. Each type of plant needs a certain amount of water, and each plant needs so many days with weather above freezing. These levels of rainfall, or precipitation, and frost-free days determine what can grow and survive. Many animals respond to plant activity. Harvester ants will not be seen aboveground gathering leaves until there are fresh leaves to be gathered. A careful eco-tracker notes what changes occur in his or her environment as warm weather arrives in the spring or the first snowfall comes in the winter. To understand these changes in weather is to see the climate in your study area.

Ecological drivers can be a constant environmental force like climate and erosion or infrequent occurrences that happen just once in five or 20 years like flood and fire. They can last for years like a drought or just a few days like a hurricane. No matter what their shape, size, or length of time, ecological drivers sculpt ecosystems. In their paths, they permit some plants and animals to survive and others to die. Within these paths, eco-trackers will find clues and signs to determine which ecological drivers changed the landscape.

Build a Weather Station

Knowing and recording weather information helps an eco-tracker keep track of environmental conditions on both a daily and a long-term basis. Although some weather stations use computers and other fancy equipment, you can build a simple weather station with just a few simple items.

To record the temperature, you will probably need a thermometer. Thermometers can be found at hardware, outdoor, and garden stores. When you set up a weather station, always read your thermometer in the same place so you can make fair comparisons about changes in temperature across time.

To measure the amount of rain, you can make a rain gauge. Use a can with the lid cut off or a wide-mouth jar that can be set out to catch falling rain. Set the container out in the open where it won't be knocked over. After a rainstorm, you can use a ruler to see how many inches (centimeters) of rain fell. When you set up your rain gauge, you can place a small layer of vegetable oil in it. The rain will fall to the bottom of the cup, and the oil will rise to the top. With the oil on top, the water won't evaporate, and you can see how much rain falls in a week or a month. If you do that, you have to remember not to measure the top layer of oil as rain when you read the rain depth.

To measure wind, scientists use an anemometer. You can use a simple flag to get a rough idea of how much wind there is and from what direction it is blowing. A small piece of fabric tied to a stick works. Write down *no wind* when the flag is still, *some wind* when the flag is flapping, and *high winds* when the flag points straight out.

Maintaining a weather station and tracking the weather is one way to monitor habitat conditions and climate change.

ACTIVITY

Rosy finches are adapted to survive in harsh and snowy conditions like the top of mountains in the western United States.

To protect both humans and wildlife, handling wild animals requires training and often involves government permits.

CHAPTER 4
Habitat and Wildlife

Raymond moved quickly. He slid open the door to the trap and reached for the small bird. He grasped the bird firmly enough to hold it but gently enough so as not to crush it. Moments before, it had been flying free, but scattered sunflower seeds lured it into the metal cage. Raymond knew right away it was a brown-capped rosy finch. He knew it as well as he knew anything. After all, he had been capturing and studying these birds since he was in seventh grade. Now an 11th-grade high school student, he was in the center of a group of biologists. They looked on as he carefully studied the animal and explained how the coloring on a few feathers made this bird a rare Hepburn's subspecies of the brown-capped rosy finch. After noting that there were no pink shoulder feathers, he further identified it as a female. His hands moved quickly and with confidence as he measured different body parts and checked the bird's health. He attached a small metal bracelet with a unique number on it to the tiny bird's right leg. He carefully passed the bird to Kobi, a nine-year-old girl, who had recorded information as Raymond processed the bird. Kobi opened her hands, and the bird returned to its wild habitat.

Raymond and his friends work with an adult bird researcher to better understand rosy finches. They study how these small birds live in some of the earth's harshest environments. Rosy finches are found in the arctic, on mountaintops, and on the edge of snowfields, where they feed on seeds and insects caught in snow. In winter, the Hepburn's gray-capped rosy finch flies south. Mostly these finches are found in the Oregon and California mountains. It's rare to see them near Albuquerque, New Mexico, at the top of a 10,000-foot (3,000-meter)-tall mountain. However, that's where Raymond and this group of young scientists found this animal. There they learn how loyal these rosy finches are to their wintering grounds. By placing numbered metal bands on these animals, they set up a method of identifying individual birds. If any bird is caught again at this location, Raymond and his friends will know which particular bird it is. This method helps them better understand how likely these birds are to return to this same spot each winter. This knowledge helps them understand how rosy finches use snow-covered mountaintops as their habitat.

Without habitat there is no wildlife. Habitat is made up of food, water, shelter, and space. For these habitat parts to be useful, their arrangement is just as important as having each of those pieces. Habitat is always larger than the animal itself.

You can think of habitat like a mountain lion on a house roof. Four walls are needed to hold up the roof. Imagine each wall as one of the key elements of habitat: food, water, shelter, and space. If any one of the "walls" is too far away from the rest, it won't hold up the roof and the lion will fall. How the habitat elements are situated is called **arrangement**.

Each animal species has particular habitat and arrangement requirements. The space a mountain lion needs might be 100 square miles (260 square kilometers) or more. A pack rat's space might be

no bigger than a soccer field. The lion's food is meat and the pack rat's mostly vegetation. The lion may need a series of rock shelters spread out over great distances and many hidden places to use to hunt prey like deer. The pack rat might only need one small crack in a rock wall to serve all of its shelter needs. Water for the pack rat might be contained in its food, while the mountain lion drinks from a stream. Habitat needs vary, but the need for habitat is universal. All creatures need habitat.

The closer you look at habitat, the more you'll see how different each section of it is. There are broad categories of habitat, like forest, field, and ocean. Each of these broad types can be further broken down into more particular types of habitat. There are cottonwood forests

and ponderosa pine forests. Even within cottonwood forests, areas are further broken down into cottonwoods with willow trees and cottonwoods with New Mexico olive trees. Each one of these habitat types supports a slightly different group of plants and animals known as an **ecological community**.

Raymond's rosy finches can't just live anywhere. They have particular habitat needs. The rosy finches are small seed-eating birds no bigger than your fist. They find their habitat in mountaintops across the western United States. In winter, they might seek better access to seeds by dropping into the lower valleys that surround mountains. As Raymond's research showed, these small birds take advantage of and survive in snowy, winter mountain habitat.

top: A backyard pond can provide wildlife with critical water.

bottom: Even a tiny puddle can provide wildlife with life-giving water.

Some animals have a narrow range of conditions in which they can survive. Others can be successful across a range of habitats and conditions. The European starling is in the second group. One hundred fifty years ago, no European starlings lived in North America. They were brought to the United States in the 1800s by someone fond of the birds, mentioned in the plays of William Shakespeare. From a small group set loose in New York, the European starling today is abundant in the 48 adjoining states as well as parts of Alaska, Canada, and Mexico. Many people who watch birds think of these starlings as "weeds of the sky." They push out native birds, congregate in noisy crowds, and take over all sorts of habitat. The European starling has a voice described in *Sibley's Field Guide to Birds* as "a mushy, gurgling, hissing chatter." This starling is rarely mentioned as anyone's favorite bird.

Favorite or not, it's an amazing creature. The European starling reminds some people of humans on this planet. It adapts to all types of habitats and makes a living under all sorts of circumstances. Even if its song isn't very pretty, it has a funny, clown-like walk that can make you laugh. Although its feathered body is rather dull, when the sun hits this bird just right, it glistens with a metallic sheen. In the world of biology, you're successful if you adapt to your habitat and raise young who then raise young of their own. The European starling is a **biological success** even if many people think of it as a loud weed with wings.

The twin stories of the European starling and the rosy finches are about habitat and survival. Animals able to take advantage of their habitat survive; those that do not die. The rosy finches adapted to the harsh conditions of ice, snow, and high mountaintops. The European starlings survived by not being too particular about where they live and what they eat.

Sometimes human actions limit an animal's opportunity for biological success. Other times animals survive because of humans. For both good and bad, humans change, destroy, and create habitat. A dam floods out a stream and destroys trout habitat, but it creates warmer, deeper water more suitable for bass.

Animals move across the face of the earth to take advantage of different and changing habitat conditions. For some, the movement is a short distance, while others cover the globe. A harvester ant stays within 80 feet (25 meters) of its nest. In one year, the sooty tern, a bird found in ocean areas, can travel in huge loops covering 40,000 miles (64,000 kilometers).

The parts of the earth where you find a species make up its **range**. Coyotes live in New York City, and they live in the Grand Canyon in Arizona. The coyote's range includes New York and Arizona because that species is found in both locations. It doesn't mean that an individual animal moves between those two places. If animals within a species routinely move back and forth between two or more locations during different seasons, they carry out an action called **migration**. Studying species movement, whether as part of an animal's range or migration, is an important part of eco-tracking. There are many citizen science programs set up to study wildlife movement. You can study the movements of just one animal, or you can study all the animals of one species in one area.

How many of a particular species there are in an area is called a **population**. The linking of animal populations is a critical part of

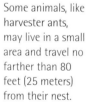

Some animals, like harvester ants, may live in a small area and travel no farther than 80 feet (25 meters) from their nest.

A pronghorn antelope can need 1,000 square miles (2,600 square kilometers) or more of habitat.

species survival. For healthy species survival, most areas of a population's habitat need to connect with each other. The places where sections of habitat link to each other allow animals the opportunity to breed, to escape temporary disturbances like a flood or fire, and to respond to habitat changes brought about by climate conditions. **Corridors** are the pathways connecting patches of habitat to each other. One of the biggest problems facing wildlife today is when patches of habitat are disconnected in what is called **habitat fragmentation**. There have always been natural causes of habitat fragmentation like rivers, islands, and even the Grand Canyon. Now roads, cities, and other human changes to the landscape have created more habitat fragmentation than ever.

You can do an easy survey of your neighborhood and look at how areas of habitat connect and how they stay separate. Sometimes you can see situations like two big parks connected by a river and the areas alongside it that are not built up. Something like this is clearly a corridor. A fence covered in vines and other plants might be both a corridor and a barrier. For small mammals like mice and shrews, it might allow passage. The fence might also block out large animals like deer and foxes. A highway is most often a barrier for both large and small animals. Across our country, roads are a major cause of habitat fragmentation.

If you travel on a road next to good habitat on a regular basis, keep track of the numbers of road-killed animals you see each month. The numbers may surprise you. Each day American cars and trucks kill 1 million birds, mammals, amphibians, and reptiles. Often these collisions cause human injuries and death as well as automobile damage. To reduce both human and wildlife losses, many people are working to make better connections between sections of habitat so wildlife can get under, over, or around human barriers like roads. One example of this change is a bridge that includes natural vegetation surfaces like bushes and grasses instead of only concrete and asphalt. Often these projects have fences to keep the animals off the highway and to funnel them across bridges or through tunnels.

Animals often are unable to survive in human-dominated landscapes.

Some of the people who decide where to put roads and other human-made features may not think very much about habitat fragmentation and the need for safe wildlife corridors. You can teach them about the need for these features by sharing your field records and mapping of wildlife roadkill and habitat fragmentation in your area. This information helps people like city and highway planners put wildlife corridors in places where they will do the most good. Before major projects like roads or factories are built, environmental plans must be made. People in the neighborhood have a chance to comment on the plans and may make suggestions, including the need for wildlife corridors in the plan. You can give your opinion and suggestions. Sometimes planners can make changes to a plan that have very little or no cost and help wildlife. It never hurts to ask. When it comes to participation in government and land planning, what matters is not your age, but the quality of your science and ideas.

top: In Albuquerque's Petroglyph National Monument, an underpass was built beneath a road to provide animals with a safe way to cross a highway.

bottom: In Albuquerque's Petroglyph National Monument, a bridge was built over a road to provide animals with a safe way to cross a highway.

Although you can watch for wildlife just about anywhere, some places offer a better chance of seeing wild animals. The best habitat is often next to and around water. Some animals, like fish and amphibians, need standing water like ponds or streams for all or part of their lives. Other animals, like many types of birds and mammals, travel to water for short periods, where they drink or seek out food or shelter.

Another excellent place to watch for wildlife is where two or more habitats come together. These overlapping habitat areas create special conditions known as **ecotones**. An example of an ecotone is where a meadow and forest come together. When these areas overlap, they create conditions not found in either the meadow or the forest. When a blob of red ink mixes with a blob of blue ink to create purple, the red and blue exist, but you find something new. The same is true of an ecotone: it's something new amid existing habitats.

When to watch for wildlife can be just as important as where to watch. The busiest times for animal activity are usually around dawn and dusk. However, even in the middle of the hottest day or coldest night, there is almost always wildlife to be seen. Watching, observing, and recording are the heart of eco-tracking.

People are often drawn to wildlife. We find wildlife to be interesting and exciting. But, in our interest to see and learn more about wild animals, we need to be **ethical observers**. That is, when we study wild animals, we must be responsible about causing the least amount of disturbance to them. If we are trying to learn about an animal and we cause it to starve to death, we are not caring for our environment. In another example, we may climb into a tree and sit next to baby birds in a nest. If we sit there for an hour, that is an hour the parents

An ecotone is where two or more habitats come together.

will not fly back to the nest and feed their young. Human presence can stop an animal from feeding and cause stress. If an animal runs away from you, it might be out of energy when it sees a real predator and needs to escape.

How we watch wildlife is more important than what we see. The first thing to remember is that wildlife is wild. It doesn't live with humans even if it lives close to humans. Respect the fact that even small, cute-looking animals can hurt you if they feel threatened.

The United States Forest Service's Nature Watch program advises people to be ethical wildlife observers. Some of their guidelines include the following:

- Observe all wildlife from a distance.
- Avoid disturbing or staying near nests and dens.
- Leave baby birds and other animals where they are.
- When viewing from indoors, turn off lights and stand back from the window so your shadow is not obvious to the animals outside.
- When you are outdoors near wildlife, move slowly and quietly.
- You can create a wildlife viewing blind by hanging dull-colored cloth with a few eyeholes cut into it and then by sitting behind it.
- The use of binoculars can help a great deal.
- If animals change behavior because you are there, you are too close. If you are in doubt, move farther away.

Let wild animals eat wild foods. With the exception of feeding back-yard birds, let wild animals find their own food. Wild animals, particularly mammals, that eat human-provided foods often get into trouble and end up having to be killed.

Responsibly record and observe what you see. If photographing wildlife, do it from a distance. Leave the habitat as you find it. Breaking branches to get a better view of a bird nest may remove the protection that keeps predators from reaching the nest. Chasing or making noises that disturb wildlife might cause the animal a loss of energy that it needs to avoid predation, find food, or otherwise survive.

Be considerate of other people. Know who owns the land you are on and ask for permission to be on private land before entering it. No matter who owns the land, follow their rules. To do so protects the wildlife, their habitat, and the visitors to that area. Pack garbage out, even trash left by someone else. All trash can harm wildlife.

Give back to nature. Find out from the local wildlife agency how to best care for animals in your area. Participate in wildlife and habitat conservation projects and help others learn how to be responsible wildlife watchers.

It's safest for both humans and wildlife if people observe wild animals from a distance by using such tools as binoculars.

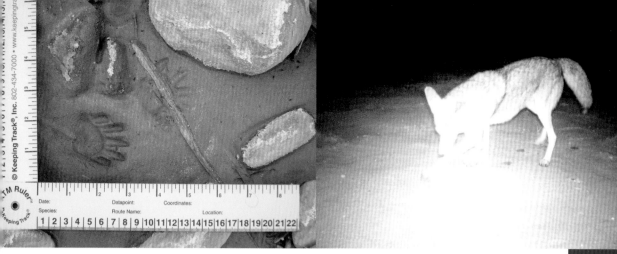

left: Observing animal tracks is an excellent way to determine what wildlife lives in a particular area.

right: Motion-sensitive cameras can reveal the wildlife in an area.

Make a Track Pit

Not all wildlife is easy to see. Sometimes the best way to determine if a species of animal exists in your area is to look for the signs it leaves. Some scientists set up motion-sensitive cameras to take pictures in the dark. Others collect hair samples and analyze them in laboratories to determine what species are present. A low-cost and effective way to determine what animals are in your area is a track pit. A track pit is just a clear patch of soil where animals walk. Each species of animal has its own track and can be identified.

A track pit can be made along a trail or in an area where other signs, like droppings or partially eaten pinecones, let you know animals are present. You can clear a patch of soil about a yard square (a meter square) of leaves, twigs, rocks, and materials other than soil. Sprinkle the soil with water and smooth it out. The soil should be damp and loose but not muddy. Test it by pushing your fingers lightly in the corner of the patch. It should leave a track with just a little bit of pressure. Leave your track pit alone overnight.

The next day, return with a field guide to tracks. You can find whole books on this subject or you can download simple track guide sheets from the Internet by typing an image request for *wildlife tracks.* As with all things related to wildlife, there are no guarantees. You may or not find tracks. When you do find tracks, make a sketch of them and record the size and how far apart the tracks are. These facts are just as important as shape when it comes to identifying the animal.

ACTIVITY

A pitfall trap is an inexpensive way to discover what insects, spiders, and other arthropods are found in an area.

CHAPTER 5
Biological Diversity

In case something jumped out of the hole, Kiyomi carefully lifted the lid away from herself. Nothing jumped. Still, the cup buried in the ground contained a mass of crawling critters. Not one of them had a backbone. There were beetles as shiny green as a new car. A centipede swirled in an S shape; although it may not have had a full comple-ment of 100 legs, it at least had dozens of them. There were insects so tiny that to truly see what they looked like would require a magnifying glass. All of these animals, and so many more, had fallen into the cup Kiyomi had buried in the ground two days before. The top rim of the cup was level with the ground; as insects and other creatures walked along the forest floor, they fell into Kiyomi's cup. Once she sorted and counted these little animals, Kiyomi would have a better idea about the different types of life found in her neighborhood forest. Her results would also become part of a larger study about the biological diver-sity, or different types of life, found in her forest.

Life comes in all different shapes and sizes. It ranges from tiny microbes smaller than the period at the end of this sentence to giant whales three times the size of a school bus. The number and types of living things found in one place is called **biodiversity**. Biodiversity is studied on many different levels. On the huge scale, it can include the whole planet. A biodiversity study can look at a part of the earth like a continent, region, or state. In Kiyomi's case, the biodiversity study covers a small area, the forest near her school.

Kiyomi's study focused on the biodiversity of only one group of animals. She just looked at the insects, spiders, and other tiny creatures with jointed legs and no backbones. These are known as **arthropods**. Arthropods are a great way to study biological diversity. First off, they tend to have very specific needs. For example, some beetles feed only on the leaves of one type of tree. Others need certain levels of soil moisture. Arthropods do all sorts of jobs in an ecosystem. An animal's or plant's job is its **niche** and how it fits into the whole community. Each arthropod has its own niche. By filling that niche, it helps the whole ecosystem stay healthy. Greater ecosystem diversity provides and maintains greater strength and health.

The contents of a pitfall trap must be handled carefully and the animals returned safely to the area where they were gathered as soon as possible after they have been identified.

To discover the arthropod biodiversity, Kiyomi did an **inventory**. In an inventory, you count the number and types of something. In this case, it was an arthropod inventory. Doing an inventory was simple, but it gave her excellent information. Kiyomi took 20 drinking cups and placed them, one at a time, into the ground. The cups made tiny pits along the surface of the ground. They became **pitfall traps**. As arthropods walked around as they always do, some fell into her cups. Kiyomi identified and counted the animals that fell into the cups. By looking closely at her pitfall traps, Kiyomi compared areas. She discovered what areas had greater biological diversity. By looking at the contents of all the cups, she looked at the biodiversity across her whole forest.

Biological diversity can also describe the differences within species. For example, within human populations differences exist among people. Some people are faster runners. Others are better at learning a foreign language. Conditions like diet and disease impact differences between every plant and animal. Biological diversity also impacts those differences. Each person, rosebush, or bit of moss, for that matter—every living thing has its own **genetic** makeup. Genetic makeup determines the possibility of what each life-form can become. A house cat's genetic makeup limits it to being a house cat. It can't grow to become a fish. Based on its diet and environment, it might grow to be four to six pounds (two or three kilograms) lighter or heavier. Its genetic makeup prevents it from growing to the shape and size of a cow. Tiny but very long strings of chemicals create the **genes** inside each life-form. The chemicals making up genes are called **DNA** (deoxyribonucleic acid). If you straightened out a string of DNA in one of your cells, it would stretch three feet (one meter) long. Inside that long string of DNA is your genetic makeup.

Within plant and animal populations, there are genetic differences. These differences help the species survive. For example, some individuals in a raccoon population are better suited for hot weather and others for cold. If the climate changes and gets hotter, the raccoon population can survive. The raccoons better suited for hot weather will thrive, while cold-weather raccoons either move to a colder area or die. In this manner, through genetic biodiversity, the species survives. There are always individual members that do not. Every species has individuals die before they are able to breed or give birth. The ones that die are sometimes just unlucky. Most of the time, those that die aren't as fit for their environment at that time and place as those that survive. An animal's fitness to survive starts with its genetic makeup.

The world constantly changes. Climate, fires, floods, and other ecological drivers are forces of change. Survival often depends on the ability to respond to changing conditions. Biological diversity is a key to a species' survival. When ecosystems change, some individuals die and some live. Those that live have the right physical abilities to survive the change. The genetic makeup and behaviors that help survival are adaptations. Biodiversity is ecological strength. It permits a population, an individual species, or even an ecosystem to live into the future.

Since biodiversity comes in so many different shapes and sizes, many different types of inventories can describe the biodiversity of a place. This includes doing a **census** of all of the different types of living organisms in a place, calculating how many of each type of organism there

Counting different species and numbers of animals, like these Canada geese, is part of doing an area census.

are in that place, and how much **bio-mass**, or total weight, of each species makes up the weight of that place.

One deer can weigh 150 pounds (70 kilograms). It would take 5 million ladybird beetles to have that same biomass. As we look into a forest, we are more likely to notice one big deer than millions of beetles and other **invertebrates** (animals without backbones) although a forest is more about invertebrates than deer. Invertebrates make up over 90 percent of forest animal biomass. They also account for most of the earth's animal biodiversity. A forest will have thousands of different invertebrate species but only one species of deer. This is why Kiyomi's study of the arthropods in her forest is so important. It's a census of that place's biodiversity.

When it comes to understanding earth's biodiversity, scientists only know a little. Less than one-tenth of the plants and animals on this planet have even been given names by scientists. By far, more is known about **vertebrate** (animals with backbones) than invertebrate species. Very little is known about the lives, habitat needs, and niches for many of the named

Although a forest has more beetles than deer, many people are more likely to notice even a camouflaged deer than a million beetles in the same area.

The biomass of five million lady bird beetles can equal one deer, yet a forest has far more biomass of beetles than it does deer.

invertebrate species. As an eco-tracker, you can still discover plenty about wildlife and habitat.

How humans benefit from biodiversity is a major study topic. The life-forms we share with the planet often keep us alive. As plants live, they make available the oxygen we need to breathe. Plants and animals are also the sources of our food supply and most medicines. For a long time, many people in the Pacific Northwest area of the United States thought of the yew tree as a giant weed. Recently, scientists found a chemical in the yew tree that can be used as a cancer-fighting drug. We don't know what plant or animal might lead us to another lifesaving drug. To destroy biodiversity is to destroy undiscovered knowledge. For very selfish reasons like these, it's a good idea to protect biodiversity.

To study biological diversity in your area, you can start with some simple steps.

First, maintain the species lists described in chapter 2. These will help you to record and track local biodiversity. An area's biodiversity changes over time as habitat changes. Your notes and lists will record that change. Take an inventory of small sections in your local environment. A smaller section used to represent a larger portion is called a **sample**. You want your samples to represent the whole area. **Representative samples** are smaller, average pieces of something larger. For example, instead of watching and recording all the seagulls at the beach, you watch only five of them. The five birds are a representative sample of all those birds. Sample size can vary, but a larger sample size makes it a more representative sample. If you watched only one seagull, it might be an odd bird. It could be sick. It may act in some other way that isn't a good example of the whole. By looking at five birds, you reduce the chance of observing odd birds.

A representative sample should be chosen without prejudice or bias. To do this, scientists use what is called a **random sample**. In the random seagull sample, any seagull was just as likely to be studied as any other. A random sample prevents you from looking at only what is close and easy to see and study.

In Kiyomi's case, she measured out 100-foot (30-meter) straight lines. Every 33 feet (10 meters), she buried a cup. This prevented her from burying cups only where it was easy to dig into soft soil. It made her collection cup placement more random. In this way, the sample was more likely to be representative and less likely to be biased. How and where she placed the cups followed an established protocol. One advantage of participation in a citizen science program is the ability to use already established protocols. When you follow the established protocols, your gathered information is easily compared with the data someone else gathered. This is true because both of you collected the information in the same way.

Kiyomi is a partner in the **Bosque Ecosystem Monitoring Program (BEMP)**. Working with BEMP, Kiyomi sends the results from her 20 traps to the University of New Mexico. Her data are added to data collected at 460 other pitfall traps that are spread out across 24 BEMP sites. All site data are collected in the same manner so scientists can compare all of the samples. It allows them to describe biodiversity across 175 miles (280 kilometers) of their state.

At her BEMP site, Kiyomi measures biological diversity in other ways too. One way she does this is with large rubber tubs. Each one is about as big around as your arms held in a circle. She places 10 tubs in her BEMP site and leaves them in place all year long. Once a month, she gathers up all of the leaves and twigs that fall into her tubs. Kiyomi then identifies, sorts, and weighs those plant parts. It lets her know what plants are in the forest. She finds which plants create and shed the most biomass. Looking at the same site over time is called **monitoring**. By monitoring biodiversity over time, Kiyomi can see changes brought about by climate and other ecological drivers.

The Bosque Ecosystem Monitoring Program involves students in gathering information about ecological conditions along the Rio Grande and its riverside forest, the bosque.

An advantage of a program like BEMP is that it is a long-term ecological monitoring program, meaning it looks at one place using the same study protocols each year. Therefore, changes over time can be detected. BEMP is just one of many monitoring programs young people can join. BEMP is part of a national **Long Term Ecological Research (LTER)** network. BEMP works with the University of New Mexico's Sevilleta LTER, which is one of many LTER stations across the country. Some are in remote areas, but many are not. In fact, one is in downtown Baltimore, Maryland. The LTER sites form a representative sample of different types of ecosystems. Each LTER site has a responsibility to teach young people about the environment. LTER sites are often great places to find scientists looking at ecosystem topics that include biological diversity, climate change, and other ecological conditions in your area. The LTER website has a special section, http://schoolyard.lternet.edu/, for young people.

A litterfall tub is just an oversized dog bowl left in one spot to catch the leaves and other plant materials that fall in a specific place in a forest.

Kiyomi won't monitor her BEMP site forever. She and her fellow students study their site for a school year, and at the end of the year, they pass their BEMP site to a new group of students. The new arrivals will follow the same protocols. Data will be collected and studied. All students, across the years, help explain their area's biological diversity and ecological changes.

Setting Pitfall Traps

Placing pitfall traps to monitor arthropods that are active on the surface like Kiyomi did is quite simple. The most important part of using pitfall traps is safety. It's more important to stay safe and to properly care for the arthropods than to collect data. Arthropod pitfall traps are just plastic drinking cups set into the ground. To place a trap, you dig a hole a little larger than the cup. Place the cup in the hole. Use one hand to cover the top of the cup and the other to scoop dirt around the sides of the cup. When you're finished, the rim of the cup should be level or just a tiny bit below ground level. A piece of wood or cardboard with a wood screw or nail in each corner can serve as a roof. Leave a few inches (centimeters) of room between the lid and the cup so small arthropods can walk under the roof. Then leave the trap alone for a day.

A pitfall trap will easily fit into the hole created by removing one shovel-full of soil.

When you return to check a trap, always lift the lid away from yourself. That way if something jumps out, it won't hit you in the face. For temporary storage and study of the arthropods that fell into the trap, you can put them into a zipper-style plastic bag. Just lift the cup by the rim out of the ground. Pour the contents into the bag, seal the bag, and quickly study and record what you found. As soon as you can, return the arthropods back to the area where they were caught. When you're done, collect the cup and trap lid, and fill in the hole with dirt.

ACTIVITY

Young citizen scientists make a difference by choosing to help the environment.

CHAPTER 6
Healing a Wounded Land

Tatianna's shovel was taller than she was. It didn't stop her, though. She handled it with all her strength. She had a job to do. With her friends, she was planting trees in a city park that had burned a year ago. They planted trees to replace those killed by the forest fire. There was no shortage of work since they were reforesting an area equaling over five soccer fields. From time to time, Tatianna's friends laughed at how much mud covered her. Tatianna looked like the ground itself, but she didn't mind. She was having fun and knew she was doing important work. Tatianna and her friends placed young trees into deep holes. As each new tree went into a hole, someone held the tree steady. Others scooped shovel loads of soil back into the hole. Each tree had a new home. Tatianna had seen to that. Across the entire burned area, Tatianna and her friends built habitat.

Look across a concrete sidewalk. Do you see habitat? You probably don't. Look closer. You may find plants pushing their way up through even the smallest crack. Perhaps a small hole in the pavement is home to an ant colony. You can find plants and animals almost anywhere.

Life is full of surprises and is an amazing force. With just a little help, wounded land can harbor wild plants and animals. The ability to come back and survive after hard times is known as being **resilient**. Nature is both fragile and resilient.

Almost everyone realizes that putting oil into a stream kills fish. Many people know air pollution damages the atmosphere. Others are aware that large sections of wild, tropical rain forests are being destroyed. These examples illustrate people's knowledge of earth's fragility. Sometimes our actions are quite severe. Some human impacts can never be corrected. This is the case when we cause a whole species to become extinct. However, not all of our actions harm the environment. Work such like Tatianna's demonstrates one example of people restoring habitat. Our planet is more than fragile. Earth's **biosphere**, or surface layer where life is abundant, is also resilient.

Life is resilient. Although ecosystems are in some ways fragile, when given just a little bit of help, even harsh or damaged areas can become good habitat.

Ecosystems as well as individual species can be resilient. By the 1970s, the American bald eagle was almost entirely gone from the lower 48 states. A chemical poison, DDT (dichlorodiphenyltrichloroethane), had been used to kill insects and was winding its way through the food chain. From farm fields and other places, DDT washed into streams and rivers. The DDT ended up in insects and waterways. It became part of the habitat. As fish swam in waterways and ate the insects, they became poisoned. When the bald eagles ate the poisoned fish, they too became poisoned. The DDT caused the bald eagle eggs to break and the young eagles within to die. Over time, fewer and fewer bald eagles remained. DDT was just one of the problems bald eagles faced. Other problems included loss of habitat and pollution. Altogether, these factors caused terrible declines in bald eagle numbers.

In recent years the bald eagle's story changed. As scientists learned about DDT's negative effects, laws were passed to prevent its use in the United States. Eagles and their habitat gained special protection under the endangered species law. It took about 25 or 30 years, but the bald eagle as a species is now doing better. Within the lower 48 states, eagles went from the edge of extinction to a healthy population. To get to this point took a great deal of human effort. The species turned out to be resilient. Once its habitat was protected and less polluted, the number of eagles grew.

Besides the bald eagle increase, there are other plant and animal species success stories. They include large and familiar animals, like the American alligator, and small and rarely known species, like the Robbins' cinquefoil, a little wild rose. Even with these achievements, many plants and animals are in harm's way. In fact, at the US Fish and Wildlife Service website (www.fws.gov/endangered/wildlife.html) over 1,200 species are listed as endangered or threatened. That means there's plenty of work to do to help nature along.

Helping wildlife and restoring habitat takes many forms. There are big projects like Tatianna's tree planting where many people work together to help wildlife and restore habitat. There are also smaller projects. If you have just a little time or money or no money at all, you can still make a difference for wildlife. Simple wildlife projects come in all different shapes and sizes.

The bald eagle is both a national symbol and an example of a species recovered from near extinction because people took care to improve its habitat and protect it. Other species can also be recovered if humans take the necessary steps to protect them.

Animals need and use water. If there are no ponds, streams, or other water sources right around your house, you can set out a bird-bath. A birdbath is just a bowl of water. Some are fancy and are sold at stores, while others are homemade. An old mixing bowl or a dog dish will do just as well. You can set your birdbath on a windowsill or on a platform in your backyard. If they need it, birds will find it. It's important to keep birdbaths clean and change the water often so diseases and pests, like mosquitoes, don't grow there.

For just a few dollars or less, you can get packets of flower seeds to plant. Many flowering plants attract butterflies and other insects and hummingbirds. Plants create shelter and food. To help wildlife, you don't need to plant a whole forest. A simple window box or out-side flowerpot filled with wildlife-friendly plants will do just fine.

Even simple things like planting seeds can create vibrant habitat for creatures like butterflies, bats, and birds.

Middle-sized projects include building bird or bat houses. These artificial homes made of wood create the shelter many birds and bats need to survive. Often their natural holes in trees are now harder to find in nature because people cut down old dead trees. Dead trees can be a safety hazard or look ugly to some people. Standing dead trees are the ones most likely to have holes in them that animals use for shelter. With dead trees being less abundant, the bird and bat boxes help make up for habitat losses. Boxes can be purchased at garden and bird-watching stores. Bird and bat box building plans can also be found on the web and in library books on wood shop projects. Many of the plans are easy to make and can be done with a few simple tools like a drill, a hammer, and a saw. For great information on how to build and place a bird box, contact the Cornell University Birdhouse network at www.birds.cornell.edu/birdhouse. The Cornell Birdhouse Network also has a citizen science program you can join to monitor the bird use of any nest box you make.

Bird boxes can replace natural cavities no longer present because of habitat loss.

To build a bat box, contact Bat Conservation International (BCI) at www.batcon.org) for plans and advice. You can join the Bat House Research Program at BCI, which collects information from people who set out bat boxes and keep track of bats.

As you make wildlife and habitat improvements around your home, you can get ideas from people who have started creating

There are many success stories when people take steps to help wildlife and heal a wounded land.

change. The National Wildlife Federation (www.nwf.org/backyard/) runs one of the best programs. Not only do they have good ideas, they also certify backyard habitats. They do that by reviewing maps and diagrams of backyards to see if they meet certain criteria for wildlife habitat. Their certification process can be done online. The National Wildlife Federation also has a program to certify schoolyard habitats. Other groups that have information about doing this type of work can be found by searching online for the key words *backyard habitat.*

If you want to do something on a larger scale to help wildlife, habitat, and the environment, you may need some help. Parks, forests, and other lands owned by the government employ rangers, biologists, and other people who care for those lands. They are almost always willing to have you help with one of their public service projects. The first Saturday of June each year is National Trails Day. This celebration includes people volunteering to work on trails. There is also a River Cleanup Week in May and Coastal Cleanup Day in September, when people work on waterways with rangers and other government officials. To find information about those projects, you can search online under the name of the program, like River Cleanup Week.

There are also many private groups working to protect the environment. They do everything from caring for injured animals to planting trees after a forest fire. To find these types of groups in your area, look in the yellow pages of the telephone book under the heading Environmental and Ecological Organizations. These groups sometimes organize special projects where young people and other citizens can do something positive for the environment.

When Tatianna was planting trees, she was part of a large project with many other people, including biologists, rangers, and even the mayor of her city. Another student was there too. His name is Thomas. In sixth grade, he learned that the cottonwood trees along the river were becoming rare. Thomas also heard about how beaver were chewing on and cutting down the cottonwood trees. Some of the government's workers wanted to kill the beaver to protect the trees, but Thomas had another idea.

Thomas believed there must be a better solution, and after thinking about it, he came up with a plan. He wanted to wrap wire fence around the base of the cottonwood trees. Thomas thought that if the cottonwood trees had a fence around them, the beaver would eat other, more abundant trees. He figured he and his friends could do the work. But before he started, he needed permission to do this work. That meant he had to go talk with the government officials

Local river and forest cleanup projects can really help improve a habitat by removing trash that could hurt wildlife survival.

who took care of the park where Thomas wanted to help. Thomas told them about his plan and that he found a business that would donate some fence for the project. The government officials said Thomas could try out his plan. After school and on weekends, he set about organizing friends and other people to protect cottonwood trees from beaver.

Over time, it became clear that Thomas's idea was a success. His work earned him some awards, including one cash prize. Thomas took the money awarded to him and put it toward a new program. He paid for a program so students in his area could visit the forest containing his cottonwood protection project and learn about beaver.

Thomas, Tatianna, Kiyomi, Raymond, Roland, Diego, and Katie are all real people. Each of them is an eco-tracker. They study, learn from, care for, and have given back to the habitat they share with wild nature. They know they are a part of the environment. Their knowledge and experiences link them to the world of plants, wildlife, and habitat.

All these young people started their work as eco-trackers and citizen scientists in middle school or earlier. Some of the things they have done are remarkable, but as people, they are normal middle and high school students.

One teen successfully started a program to protect cottonwood trees from beaver by wrapping the trees with wire fence. This also saved beaver from being killed because people did not want beaver to eat cottonwoods.

Some got good grades while others did not. A few of them have gone to college. Every one of them went through hard times and faced tough obstacles in life. What each of them did on his or her path to becoming an eco-tracker and citizen scientist was to connect with the wild world and take care of it.

It doesn't require a college degree or a certain age to be an eco-tracker and citizen scientist. All it takes is a willingness to look around outside. The environment is right where you are. Something is happening. There are plants and animals surviving right outside your door. So get up. Get out. Go see what's going on in your wild neighborhood. Learn about and care for your own little corner of the earth. You are an eco-tracker and citizen scientist and you can make a difference.

Citizen scientists create a healthier world for people and wildlife.

Joining Forces for a Better Environment

There are always habitat and environment projects that need your help. You can be like Tatianna and help out with a project set up by someone else. Or you can be like Thomas and think of some part of the environment in your area that needs help and then make a plan to work on it. In either case, you need to work with the landowner. Sometimes the landowner is some type of government like a city or state. Other times a person, people, or company might own it. No matter who owns the land, you must have their permission to change it. This is true even if what you want to do will help the land and its wildlife.

If you aren't sure where to do this type of work or who you need to ask, you can contact a local wildlife or forestry department. Ask to speak to someone in the education, public information, or outreach department. The people in those jobs are used to working with young people. There are also national programs like Project WILD and Project Learning Tree that have people in almost every state ready to help young people care for the environment. If you want to take care of the environment, there are always projects and people who need your help.

One person, no matter his or her age, can make a difference.

ACTIVITY

Further Information

First of all, get outside. Spend as much time as you can outdoors learning about the environment firsthand. City parks, schoolyards, backyard bird feeders, and all the other places we share with wildlife and the rest of nature are the most important part of citizen science and eco-tracking. When it's time to come inside, the following websites can help you on your path toward becoming an eco-tracker and citizen scientist.

The **Audubon Society**, with its annual Christmas Bird Count and other activities, has one of the oldest and largest citizen science programs. www.audubon.org/bird/citizen/index.html

The **Bosque Ecosystem Monitoring Program (BEMP)** is an example of a statewide citizen science environmental project. www.bosqueschool.org/bemp.htm

The **Citizen Science Projects'** website is a general introduction to and directory of citizen science projects of all types. www.citizensci.com

The **Citizen Weather Observer Program** helps people track weather and climate conditions in a scientific manner. www.wxqa.com

Cornell University's Lab of Ornithology runs several of the best citizen science programs related to birds. www.birds.cornell.edu

GLOBE is an international monitoring program that allows young people and others to gather environmental data in their area and then share their results on the Internet. www.globe.gov

The **Long Term Ecological Research (LTER)** network has special projects related to global climate change and other topics for young people. www.lternet.edu. In that website go to schoolyard.lternet.edu.

The **National Wildlife Federation** provides information on creating backyard wildlife habitat in either small or big steps. www.nwf.org/backyard

Project Learning Tree (PLT) at www.plt.org and its GreenWorks' partnership and **Project WILD** at www.projectwild.org support young people working on environmental-enhancement projects. PLT and Project WILD are also a good source of information for young people about the environment. Each of the programs has a coordinator in almost every state and several different countries to help young people care for the environment.

Glossary

accurate: A description that does not have mistakes.

adaptation: A change over time that helps an animal or a plant survive or not survive under certain conditions.

area list: A description of all the different species found in one place.

annual list: A description of all the different species found in one year.

arrangement: How a variety of items are found near one another.

arthropod: An animal with jointed legs but no backbone, like an insect or a spider.

bias: A prejudice that prevents scientific information from being properly recorded.

biodiversity: A description of all the living plants, animals, and other organisms found in a place.

biological success: Describes if a plant, an animal, or another organism has been able to reproduce.

biomass: The weight of either an individual or a group of organisms.

bioregion: A description of a large area that has common characteristics.

biosphere: The layer of the earth where life is concentrated.

bosque: The Spanish word for *forest*; it is used in New Mexico to describe a riverside forest.

Bosque Ecosystem Monitoring Program (BEMP): A citizen science monitoring project where students and others study the Rio Grande and its riverside forest.

census: To count all of one type of item in an area.

citizen science programs: Research projects where young people and others without formal science education can assist in a scientific study.

climate: The long-term weather conditions in an area.

community (ecological): The plants, animals, and other features that make up an ecosystem.

corridor (wildlife): A place in nature where animals can move back and forth between two different habitats.

daily list: A description of all of the species observed in one day.

data: The information collected about a particular condition or situation that can often be shown with numbers.

data forms: Special charts designed to record information.

desertification: A situation where an already dry ecosystem turns into a desert (often because humans overuse the land).

DNA (deoxyribonucleic acid): The chemical that makes up genes.

ecological community: The living and non-living elements that make up the environment in one particular area.

ecological drivers: Forces that act on the environment and cause change.

ecosystem: Both the living and non-living parts of an environment that interact with each other to create habitat.

ecotones: Where two different types of habitat come together and create a third.

eco-tracker: Someone who studies environmental change.

environment: Everything in a particular area.

environmental footprint: The measurement of someone or something's impact on the earth in terms of items like energy, food, water, and pollution.

erosion: Where the earth wears away because of wind and water.

ethical observers: People who attempt to disrupt nature as little as possible as they watch it.

exotic: Something that is not native and has come from someplace else.

field guide: A book that helps to identify plants, animals, or other parts of nature.

field notes: A written record of what a scientist or eco-tracker observes in the out-of-doors.

genes: Made of DNA, they provide the instructions in each living organism that defines its body.

genetics: The study of how organisms inherit their characteristics from their parents.

global climate change: How long-term weather conditions across the planet are different over time.

habitat: The physical location where a plant or animal lives, consisting of food, water, shelter, and space.

habitat fragmentation: A condition in the environment where ecosystem sections are disconnected from each other, often because of human activity like road building.

inventory: To count all of a particular species or item in a certain area.

invertebrates: Animals, like insects and spiders, that don't have backbones.

life list: A list of all the different species that one observer records throughout his or her life. Often the life list focuses on a type of plant or animal like birds.

Long Term Ecological Research (LTER): A worldwide system of research stations that study global climate conditions, changes, and related topics.

micro-view: To look at an area up close and on a small scale.

macro-view: To look at an area in a broad way and on a large scale.

migrate: To move from one place to another and back again on a regular basis.

monitoring (environmental): Studying a particular condition, like weather or pollution, over time.

naturalist: Someone who studies nature.

niche: The job or function that an individual plant or animal fulfills within its ecosystem.

pitfall traps: Cups, buckets, or other containers that are set into the ground so that walking animals will fall into them.

population: A particular group of something, often living in the same area.

precise: To be exact in describing something.

protocols: A set of procedures followed the same way each time a specific task is done to maintain quality research.

random sample: A smaller part of a larger group where any of the larger group's members could have been selected to be in the small group.

range: An area where something can be found.

representative sample: A smaller, average piece of something larger.

resilient: The ability to come back and survive after hard times.

sample: A small part of something used to represent something larger.

species: A particular type of plant or animal that is able to have offspring like itself who are in turn able to have offspring of their own.

species list: The record of different types of species one observer sees.

sustainable living: The ability to live in one place over an indefinite time.

vertebrate: An animal with a backbone, like a mammal or bird.

Welcome to

Worlds of Wonder

A Young Reader's Science Series

Advisory Editors: David Holtby and Karen Taschek

In these engagingly written and beautifully illustrated books, the University of New Mexico Press seeks to convey to young readers the thrill of science as well as to inspire further inquiry into the wonders of scientific research and discovery.

Illustration Credits

Index

73; and the Arctic, 7; definition of, 76; as an ecological driver, 26, 28, 36, 59. *See also* global climate change

Coastal Cleanup Day, 68

community, 54; definition of, 76; ecological, 42; and habitat, 11; sustainable, 10. *See also* ecological community

Cornell University Birdhouse Network, 67. *See also* citizen science programs

Cornell University Lab of Ornithology, 73

corridor, 45, 46, 47; definition of, 76

cottonwood, 27, 31, 42; as habitat, 5; protection of, 69, 70; survival of, 21

daily list, 20; definition of, 76. *See also* species list

data, 20, 21, 59, 60, 61, 74; data forms, 21, 76; data logger, 15; definition of, 76

DDT(dichlorodiphenyltrichloro-ethane), 64, 65

desertification, 35; definition of, 76

digital sound recorder, 15

DNA (deoxyribonucleic acid), 55, 77; definition of, 76

drought, 30, 35, 36

Earthship Biotecture community, 10. *See also* sustainable living

ecological community, 42, 54; definition of, 76

ecological drivers, 26, 56, 59; definition of, 76; and habitat, 27–36

ecosystem, 6, 7, 19; BEMP and, 59, 60; biological diversity and, 54, 56, 64; connections to, 24, 28; definition of, 76; ecological drivers of, 31, 32, 36

ecotones, 47, 48; definition of, 76. *See also* habitat

eco-tracker, 1–5, 9, 14–18, 21–24, 32, 35–37, 58, 70–73; definition of, 77

environment, 1, 2, 6, 9, 10, 11, 13–25, 40, 55, 56, 58, 71, 73; caring for, 48, 62, 64, 68, 69, 72; changes to, 7, 8, 28, 32, 35; connections to, 70; definition of, 77; environmental footprint, 8, 9, 10, 11, 77; and the GLOBE program, 19; and habitat, 3, 5; and LTER, 60

erosion, 28, 29, 32, 35, 36; definition of, 77

ethical observers, 48; definition of, 77

exotic, 31; definition of, 77

field guide, 18, 20, 43, 51; definition of, 77

field journal, 16, 35

field notes, 14, 15, 22; definition of, 77

genes, 55; definition of, 77

global climate change, 2, 19; definition of, 77; and LTER, 60, 74, 78

Global Learning and Observations to Benefit the Environment (GLOBE), 20, 74

gray-capped rosy finch, 40

habitat, 1–11, 20, 28, 33, 34, 37, 57, 58; definition of, 77; fragmentation, 45–47, 77; restoring, 63–70, 72; types of, 35; and wildlife, 39–50, 65

human-dominated landscapes, 46

inventory, 55, 58; definition of, 77

invertebrates, 57; definition of, 78

Long Term Ecological Research (LTER), 60, 74; definition of, 78

macro-view, 21–22; definition of, 78
micro-view, 20, 21; definition of, 78
migration, 2, 44; definition of, 78
monitoring, 59, 60; definition of, 78

National River Cleanup Week, 8
National Trails Day, 68
National Wildlife Federation, The, 68; definition of, 74
naturalist, 14, 16, 19, 20, 24; definition of, 78
New Mexico, 10, 30, 40, 42; University of, 59, 60
niche, 54, 57; definition of, 78

pitfall traps, 55, 59, 61; definition of, 78
ponderosa pine forest, 30, 31
population, 44, 45, 55, 56, 65; definition of, 78; human, 55
Project Learning Tree, 72
Project WILD, 72
protocols, 20, 21, 59, 60; definition of, 78

representative sample, 58, 60; definition of, 79

resources, 9
Rio Grande Valley, 31
River Cleanup Week, 68
roadkill, 46

sample, 58–60; definition of, 79. *See also* representative sample
scientific investigation, 14
Sibley's Field Guide to Birds, 43
solar energy, 10
species list, 20, 58; definition of, 79
sustainable living, 10, 11; definition of, 79

Taos Pueblo, 10. *See also* sustainable living

US Fish and Wildlife Service, 65

vertebrate, 57; definition of, 79

weather station, 37
wildlife, 38, 70, 71, 73, 74; corridors for, 46, 47, 76; and habitat, 40, 42, 58, 68; movement of, 44; observing, 47, 48, 49, 50, 51; problems facing, 45; protecting, 65, 66, 67, 68, 69, 72; refuge, 41; tracks of, 51